Ladies & Gentlemen

Michael Robins

saturnalia books

Distributed by University Press of New England
Hanover and London

Saturnalia Books
105 Woodside Rd.
Ardmore, PA 19003
info@saturnaliabooks.com

ISBN: 978-0-9833686-0-1
Library of Congress Control Number: 2011934348

Book Design by Saturnalia Books
Printing by The Prolific Group, Canada

Cover Art: Lithograph by Adolph Friedlander, Stichting Circusarchief Jaap Best
www.circusmuseum.nl

Distributed by:
University Press of New England
1 Court Street
Lebanon, NH 03766
800-421-1561

Grateful acknowledgment is made to the editors of the following journals where versions of these poems (occasionally with different titles) first appeared: *AGNI*, *Bateau*, *Columbia Poetry Review*, *Conduit*, *Crazyhorse*, *Denver Quarterly*, *Handsome*, *Horse Less Review*, *Indiana Review*, *InDigest*, *Jet Fuel Review*, *LUNA*, *MAKE*, *Order & Decorum*, *Ploughshares*, *Route 9*, and *TYPO*.

"[What light in the sky to leave, what flags]" appeared as a limited-edition broadside created by Evan Commander as part of the Moor Reading Series, 2007. "In the Manner of All Such Disasters" appeared as a limited-edition broadside created by Michael Dunn as part of the Poets in Print Reading Series at the Kalamazoo Book Arts Center, 2009.

Circus first appeared as a chapbook by Flying Guillotine Press, 2009.

Table of Contents

for Valerie

A circus passed the house—still I feel
the red in my mind though the drums are out.

—Dickinson

I

Sleep Is Not Unlike a Waiting Room

The dead deer is more alive to you now
than reclined, early September, eyes lit

in the chill shadow of the cherry tree.
The dead deer is more alive to you now

than the featherless bird without a nest.
Neither do you claim by the happiness

of plans, dropping your pencil to the floor
as if to ask what it means to scrape skin

crudely, pushing a child until he bleeds.
You too think frequently of the jumpers,

whether any stole for the arms of god
or if only the sky, the blue it's said

that seemed to ring the smoke like a halo.
Like gypsum, like horses leaving those birds

splayed, to fall must have felt like flying,
jaspers in exchange for the body's flesh.

Like rifles falling with the sun, flying
like chorus. You took photos of the deer

by which I mean you blinked a broken thing
lying there, a bruise of wrinkle & dust.

The dead deer is more alive to you now
than childhood. To wonder why you weren't

saying much, not unlike his awful shirt,
thought like a caption for the falling man.

What I Was Doing About the War

Therefore the moment materialized,
bad luck. It was the dog no one heard

who barked for that question split,
pretext in the sand around a convoy.

A small boy rolled his tire with a stick:
smoke signal, telepathy, the satellites

that pin the speck of beauty to a point.
The question tore a sleeve with light.

It was no longer poetry, rather instance
for a mutual subtraction to thrive.

Rhetorical, it was the cruelest music.
Whatever cry turned to explanation,

the mourning dove alone struck clean
like glass. It was weather & forecast,

too true to move against countrymen:
handsome, then across the periphery

a hand like a question in the sun. Also,
the stubborn mule tied to a sad piano.

After Gordon Matta-Clark

—for Joel Craig

I understood, terrible for those names
of friends as though a kindly bleach released

my apprehension, so many windows
for so many stones. Floor beams devour

our head, handsaws our hand & so pronounced
the efflorescence willing for the world.

What did it mean to feel? If love propels
the air, the boy within gapes back on you.

Absence feeds his house, lit like your kidney
carried down a stairwell sawn in two.

I had the astonishment on the mend,
floating there, meaning I owned a face

abandoned for the wrecking ball. I'm keen
on the warren that perforates this room.

Air could pass as easily through our lives
as a blemished food that fills with brightness.

The Birds of Massachusetts Bay

Falling asleep is dangerous. Each night
the wilds scatter our quiet fire, relentless

to the wooden flesh of this early town.
Doors line up in every hall, so written,

no pigs involved. News is not adequate,
let alone malnourished words part cloud

in a lake no less cloud. We, first settlers,
can't believe misfortune for our spades

are unaccounted. We'd take the gulls
if our arms could hold steady: we frighten

them away, poor scarecrows of the beach.
Our child drifts thoroughly in a draft

contained by the shore. Every ship a ship
too late, our thin blankets ill, mornings

we spread them well to the kind people
of the new country. Watch over us, Lord,

our Loot, our Load as winter settles in.
Our song, our only song, is lofty as flame.

Somewhere I Have Heard This Before

To convey the story wrong, likely said
from the gate into water this horse strayed

toward dusk. I've heard this lake is happy
like a funeral, resuming where its source

retreats. Year on year I remember the hinge,
the winding key for the horse. Then I wind

these horseflies, fields which from below
appear forlorn. Many speak now of flight,

the towering walls. You say I scraped by
with kindness, in railed hues, but I never

hear the horses coming. Saying goodbye
I say nothing, like this wall I muster.

What can I suggest to the trees, in tune
to the sky one morning? I wind airplanes

for their engines deliver some distance
from cities. I've heard that lakes disappear

to confuse assurance, saying at times
I left the trees, bloodshot, in the surface.

They shine through the lake into the sea,
no appetite for grass. What do I say,

what passes to dirge for anyone? This way
I speak you'd guess the world is mostly wall,

mostly wall when saying mostly water.
You say I never see the horse swimming.

Between Us Now Bends the Mississippi

If I bridge a river, you fade away. Not
cutting in line for groceries, for green

by the mule & plow on a distant shore.
Chandelier, glasslamp wavering to wave

goodbye. Of that joy I remember none
so much as October, your burning home,

every feeling in the photographs posed
like teacups of air. Your face is not pulp,

not oranges nor pears, nor is your body
like scissors pruning trees. Like a lantern

adheres each morning to the lifting fog,
this is your light. This will be your light.

All Our Pretty Songs

The pale horse rises steadily, again
like any funneled rage to fire clay.

Of those praying among the murals
at Labská Týnice, I'm attracted most

to Anna's mother. She plays perfect
accordion. She is fragments of bread

that could lead me to love. To love,
we acknowledge too those spectacles

in the field: the headstones, the teeth
taken for their gold. I know in winter

I've been to Prague, but I am young
for taking Anna's hand, for her hand

is the invitation of which only the year
she understands. We will converge

in that year, which will be known
for branding the pale horse Anna:

she's the one who filches my breath.
I can feel her blaze before she dances.

A Terrific Descent Through Space

If the heavens & hell are here on earth,
trains appear, reappear amid the hills

like spilled milk, no animal in the sky
save a whirlwind, save the neighborhood

stolen from the ash like a second skin
molting, mounted over the autumn blue.

All the time I'm licking language, letters
posted inside envelopes for someone

yet stranger than words, exquisite ringing
still in the bell approaching the station.

First kissing, undressing an old address
before you knew how the river misses

no more silver coins. Cigarettes only,
homeliness like pigeons in the warm glow

only magnified, new embers vowing
what I'd wanted, all along, to convey:

like a train you stared into the sunrise.
Every fruit, rather, wasting in the trees.

Stuck in My Mouth Like a Bit

The days were awful. Isn't this awful?
We say as much, in truth we pointed north

seasonably, the sun as a moment
we would in some way fail, eventually

awoken from this muscled arm of land.
Like the needle in hay, our direction

on the road into the sea, What curled
under the surface? Who held out a hand?

To repeat the awful welcome: the sun,
the breeze, we speak loosely of memory

for memory now like salt over sand,
our barrel chests like Charlton Heston's

if that way is north. From crevice to web,
we blanket the oasis of beachfront.

We came from that north temporarily,
heads adrift like the seals along the shore.

Melissa gathered stone for her daughter,
from water some cheer. For the piano

now lost to the sea, forgotten nearly
we would sing, awfully all we would sing.

Whose lips said north? If that way is north
we were magnets for a portrait of pigs,

hay ahead of stick, the hair of their chins.
We run, a kite's string pitching to the blow.

Was the piano that awful? Creeley
listened from the cradle of her mother

snug, her voice crooning north to Canada
to echo for this reunion of friends.

True north stood in a crib, not so distant
her crawl, her little step across our tongue.

Your Voice Is as Much a Kind of River

If at night the rain slips past, I saw you.
You were home. Your taxi from the airport

rolled over the dog & I think the dog
never made it long. What are the chances?

It was enough that others believe me
in your company. This is how I came

seeking lamb, hours in a plastic bag
coaxed like so & salvaged in the darkness.

In Tennessee stands a billboard that reads
Redneck Steakhouse. Never so happily

did I hobble the hills, an awkward drum
hung within my chest: there's to be mostly

pained music, or else river. Or else now:
that dog runs freely through a good evening,

the chance rock floating off the overpass
vanished like intention. Like glint on grass

but ruinous, more intimate than friends
who have fallen at once through the same air.

Hundreds of men floated over these falls.
Of those who were suicides, a handful

survived. You are waiting & dripping wet,
staring as if through the clouds to the stars.

Moments Went Missing Thanks to Whiskey

I fell, which is something I sometimes do
when poisoned. Like birdhouses & beggars,

when I fall some time elapses. I rose
like sod from the sidewalk, like a barn owl

from some carnage of a red folded field
or broken bones, stacked by an empty shed.

My raindrops took days to repair. When I
sunk like a pear, I was the proof that fell.

I was not cool, steady like a sport coat
bloated on mammals & thinking theorems.

I fell, which is something I sometimes do
when singing. Like a bird's nest washed asea.

I Wanted More Than I Could Steal

Instead the opening, the tunnel, the end
through which breath turns to wood.

Animals shoulder the glossy, pubescent
luster. There, between the stacked pages

& the clean press of our jeans, the future
is a passage closing in pornsong. There

you dig, you cover the space with moss.
You anticipate your meals like a spider.

Arrival is not the great seizure of hands
devoted pure, & we could not always save

the pages from rain. A shy introduction,
our smiles startle lovers, so simplistic

the scenery as we descend the new valley.
Are we asleep or has this too expired,

exits without meaning? Worldly a week,
we browsed our magazines: this explains

the absence of skin, our softness so great
we please the day steaming south. Nothing

of our eyes, which continue as a corridor
continues. We're sleeping, we're asleep,

we mouth our wet trampoline, white legs,
white thighs, a plea of white cotton there.

You, who could be so cruel & not simply
in our dreams. For this we look as looking

to our god: we're worldly, we are weak.
Pornography explains an unhappy paging

of our hands, our smiles now boats adrift
in the harbor. From the harbor our train

leaves to sidle the coast. Limbs & loins,
they know nothing of tides nor the surge.

& you in the early gloss, not at the station,
no flowers when our train does not arrive.

Off the Shoulder of Orion

In the music box these organs smile
dumbly, a thumb, a thumb to fontanel

like a metronome. Like is it not safe
anymore to conceive the unicorns?

If we turn a key the finch will rotate,
sing ideas like a tumbrel end to end

into fields where I find a hair to keep
me awake & staring through the closure.

Like no maker makes if he tries only
to remember the road from the airport.

To remember the road from the airport
like musical chairs without any chairs

or music, no timbre building a nest
beyond the enigma that leads it home.

Time will tune a tooth in a music box,
cylinder through which I left a thread

to follow. Like a source for a picture,
like a milky skin that settles each thing.

Mended Sonnet

Whitsun, it was that elegance. It was
doubtless, less of the tree line evident

when we were living in it. Drunkenly
reckoned over end, hanging by the ledge,

you never broke every bone in your hand.
Equation was neither a friend. Neither

suture, a picket fence absolved like flesh.
It was, in lieu of Sunday, the instance

leaving its name behind. Listing it was.
Nurtured, the last fish we ever caught

refusing the boat like a remainder.
It was our residence in drag. It was

chanced upon, wistful as a flower spent.
Like a part you missed, you've already left.

Living Statues on Horseback

Am I a pedestrian, best foot forward,
or am I grass? Along the highways

I let pass the '90s, the white, roadside
cross enclosed by roses, roses, roses.

The lyrics of my last favorite song
betray the sentiment of their chords

& low beams, the single procession
toward the tarpaulin of the cemetery.

In the miles between here & Missouri,
the billboard I say aloud is the one

that reads Jesus. Later, not too later,
I hear my song on the advertisement

for cars, the notes & words hammered
like death to the ground. Am I stuck

in breathing or am I shrub? The sun,
which also rises, ignites the horizon

before us, crows truncate the radiance.
Sometimes those wayward engines fly.

His Passion Is Doves

During the bombing, the man fills his truck
with lumber, which is later used to make men

who fill the truck with brick. The sawdust
washes from his brow to shore, a recess

beyond the mirrored flash of the lighthouse
where we meet as if in a camp. We're drunk

& happy, awaiting arrival of a luminous bride
around whom we would join hands & sing.

Bewildered, our pigeons flew ashore long ago.
They mull the rooms of old, coastal motels,

the mirrors of which are filled with bicycles,
pedals turning no one behind their bells.

During the bombing, the man fills his truck
with lumber, despite our singing. It's used

to make men who stack his truck with loam.
Should he love, our idea of love must end.

A Modern Production

If I kissed you before we held hands, no matter. I'm hugging Elmore, collector of things precious, convex, things written & referenced from a recipe box. Though I dream in bed beside you, I want to write you a letter: all around the porcelain dolls attend like good soldiers. If a comic strip imitates life, life hangs on the refrigerator with magnets. My thanks, dear Elmore, for these things delicious. In one photograph her husband tan, toned beside her, standing on his hands. Everyone all around smiling. Eventually, I'm told, his heart would implode.

Ideas of Maryland

We paved roads that they might travel
& so traveling, reproduce. In these days

no taste is spared, these days los lobos,
my hours deliberate as script upon skin.

In the idea captive with smoke, the sky
fastens Maryland's seasons, its scrawl

the piled leaves. New to such rapture,
we stay in line to better heed the sound,

we draw pictures to match our feelings.
It's a full note in Maryland's jeans I prefer

to work, the idea of pleats in Key West.
Maryland's our yacht, tethered & taut,

ivy grown where no one lusts. We had
had the advice of others, now we've none.

We arrive or flee from our clouded plans:
they're rabbits, they're ideas lent to a dog.

If roads can kill, could they not partner too
& mate for life? The road, another road

we never travel, but our idea of Maryland
is beautiful: orioled, leaves a little gently

& the banner for the best year of our lives.
In these days more ivy, more women who

follow wolves. In turn we follow pastel
from the trees into tiny, black-eyed daisies.

We are no longer the young apprentice,
dazzling & zealous. We dub this los lobos.

Each day we draw we respond to Maryland,
to rainfall, nothing of the plums, so heavy

in our pockets. I think we'd rather die
than uncover a child to reign this world.

Peaceful in the Loving Arms of Jesus

Or else the sheets are empty of the bed
by which we floated clean. We didn't die

from mercury, ascending like voices
bred in the years of the world behind us.

Neither are we makings of a band, not
sunrise beyond any span long with time.

Neither are levees stowing fine china
from sleep, New Orleans like a refugee.

We hadn't time for pelicans diving
peaceful, from the longing arms of Jesus

to the waters of the flooded streets.
Death went missing in my empty wallet

but that is not here, not yet some smiling
from our casket left broken in the sun.

For how long will desire like smiling
balance, crossing this wire to reach us?

Quietude Puts Me in the Doghouse

Within a blur, you kneel within a hold
of water. Forewarned, memory obscured

like a part of speech rowing from the shore.
Before long we've worn a bed together,

memory adorned: Hi, you say. Hello…
Of the various things in life some thought

is important, one early dead soldier
tightly reined, anchored suddenly to blaze.

Perpetual, his clear blue eyes are gauze.
Language flails after the boy, your silence

like smoking, like clouds over a small town.
Here is one kind of war: I hated you

less than I loved myself for hating you.
Season poor in weather, my substitute

basking in the shade of an empty beach.
Within that cloud a less visible cloud.

We Are Standing Momentarily

Exact change, migrations downstream
to verify Missouri, part frigid in the dusk

like so many clothes on a bearskin rug.
As some can never not dance, someone

leads all the enemy to the dogwoods,
their red leaves in a velvet covered sky.

Once I fell knowing well I wouldn't fly,
three blossoms in the branch above me.

As some birds feed in Missouri's smile
some neighbors breed wolves: moonlit,

a chorus of damned women in the mist,
they gnaw through closed screen doors.

My hearth was once too bright for two:
accordingly, I will never play the tuba.

I won't frolic nor do I parade to witness
lapping from a cold, metal bowl. I nest

to greet any flicker without this shame.
No flower, no sight but that in the trees

festooned with cardinals, red berries
& often dancing. Missouri's is the large,

bashful hand fastened to a private man.
No wonder the stars burn on without us.

Bit by a Dog with a Rabid Tooth

In the waiting room there are no clocks
available, a trend we noted in parlors

for the dead. One needs ambience, one
an ear sewn back to its starting position.

The new arrivals are first to be called:
this fills our hearts, spreads a theory

like bacteria surveying the Aztec people.
One goes absent over a year. Voiceless,

tenants are discovered in her womb:
feathers, oxygen found only in the well

of a newborn's lung, that small drum
for small thumbs. Some say that's code,

it might hail the triumphs of Cortez.
Some that it resembles a conquistador

delivered from the straw that flared
down the road, home after home. Names

are drawn from the mahogany barrels,
friends are led to a second waiting room:

in that way they'd eat apples in Spain
& shortly be heading home. For being

so good we choose two of the following:
manzanos, towels & gauze, an account

of Hernando's conquest, his quiet end.
None will be erased quite so by autumn.

Anne Kepler Come Home

In the closet Rothko leans so much like an angel, I can't say if art imitates Russia
or Russia imitated art. The cat tips the glass for a little water, the surge of the
season catches even the flautist off balance. Though you are sleeping now beside
me, your wings furled, I want to send you this letter: we are too far from Tulsa to
get there by Christmas, among the trees there are lights far fewer than last year.
At night I variously dream, including a plume through the open fields of Latvia.
When I ask each morning, no one will acknowledge ever knowing a flautist.

When It Snows in Boston It Snows Everywhere

To brand our memories of a far land
like sunrise, like a whetstone in the barn

of narrowing fog. If the slow dancer
in me is smaller than a thunderstorm,

I leave my watch alone, near a mirror,
each morning thinking often of our bed.

By harbor, by sea, by the breakwater's
shine, now is the time perfect for marriage,

a miracle that one could maybe love
enough: wooden owl in the wooden sky,

memento reassured like Queen Anne's lace
replacing the safe behind the painting

of the safe. If you believe a fish feels
disappointed when it gets caught, indeed

either way I look. Your hand in my hand,
we love, we name our failure of orchids

like we might souvenirs, statues slipping
deeply through the water after moonlight.

I'll assume no quiet way to leave you
this note: Will you marry me? Be my wife.

III

Circus

*If destruction be our lot, we must
ourselves be its author and finisher.*

—Lincoln

What light in the sky to leave, what flags
through town, their white Qs. How I was

as I had been has nothing against captains,
with distance between an awkward door

& fence, in what appear to be the stars
in a month in this string of deadly months.

My movement upends, my gestures vanish.
This happens again & again like lightning

to rod. Like difficult to stand if standing
is stance, the wedge between citizen & me.

Where Q gets buried I found this string
& pulled. Doing so, could not stop pulling.

Our casualties I hear precede the smoke,
in a bed of snakes. There can be no rain

in America, no grass; trains are angry here
as some are sad, processional for an ear.

The Q drums momentum, helluva cannon
in that sound. Helluva trumpet nesting.

To acknowledge my mistress of writhing:
what knife when thrown that does not sink

through wood nor perish from the earth.
I answered the roll call, the country carried

closely in our chests. Tell me what ring,
what insurgency, what thrust so extreme.

I held out my hands at length, a still life
of flesh & string. Consider the imperative

knowing better to grieve, falling that lands
some nurture. Q, dear friends, begins again

for our secretary retreats behind his ax.
Write a letter & stop it for the river, leave

the voice inside a bottle when you stand
before the ledge with a dog, a small hand

in your hand. Alone, I deliver somersaults
for you. If sometimes I'm turning song,

if instead my fingers build a cradle empty
in the tent filled with air, with breathing.

I bought a blue shirt & called it ours, a Q
but no one asked. What allegiance to the year

I lifted a glass so fully to the wedge, animals
like questions standing tall before the war

on the train. Describe a man of description
& the man vanishes from the astonished ring.

We go home to our beds, sleep softly. We
dream a living statue who dreams of fortune,

the fight, the flag. If one train leaves St. Louis
& another leaves Chicago, find me a captain

who makes no baby cry. Fabric or wood,
stow the Q to fuel these hours with answers.

Q burned like a stick, like a brick it fell.
The wind, it blew our clothes. My captain

rides a saddle he calls principle, foolish
to you like flute, flue or flurry. For me

it began on a train, I didn't sleep, oh well.
For me in flurry it wasn't love. Questions

in the night passed our window like horses,
their forms a brilliant reflection: water

was to music as _____ was to war.
Q burned like a building filled with paper,

I regret to inform the whistle of your lips.
Pursuant of praise, my captain buries men.

For every blade of grass, for every name
removed to stone the Q. Shot through,

air shot through. I wished to save the one
who'd fallen before us, the astonishing feat.

I'm on a train. I'm on a train to work
far from the stony ridge obscured in light.

For a time I left the interior scene, what
nesting-place surrendered for the curtain,

greatest show from my seat. Such comfort
I opened the flue, thought like a blue shirt.

To breathe full measure beneath some trees,
to reign supreme in the serpent kingdom.

Q in itself is not heaven, nor is lakefront
nor a circus. Of all the camels none balance

on a leg in the train passing by. Soldiers
sleep standing on their feet: not an acrobat,

they are figures each for doppelgangers.
I was a boy, laying out my best blue clothes

to be better seen with Q, my captain
in a room shining shoes like the world's

most terrifying creature. A circus is not god,
nor is the menagerie, nor will those dead

train for war anymore. I forget such wars.
I beam, leave the young me sleeping, asleep.

When each letter woke it entered a tunnel
for the wreckage of the world. Q took fire

for the fallen Q, I was a bush but I was not
burning. Yes, Q rode a camel to the store

& returned with a wedge & its sad parade.
Or a flag with a few less stars. I didn't speak

but grimaced like a supreme test of merit.
Not a summer evening, nor did the voices

come to pass. Q rides a camel to the store
but that is not all we heard of Q. All day

I stand inside the city's only movie house,
which is also this pile of cinder & bricks.

Step right up for my captain speaks slowly,
heartsome, declared in lieu of Q. A flute

is not like fluency: one covets enemies
drawn from the earth & swung, & neck.

If shadow conquers light, if in the first ring
is a white house, then in the second ring

a stand of donnybrook, of hum, of convoy.
Now we are engaged in a great civil war:

the balloon conveys this perfect harmony.
It's a fine day, really. My captain declares

like all the world is strung inside a piano,
as though every hammer produces song.

What amazement in sound, what marvel
acts when the door opens on the congress

of fathers in my chest. The clowns, some
of whom of course wore Qs, obscured

those eyes in attendance. Acrobats swung,
animals showed almost human intelligence

& reason. To address the first of many letters
to my captain, to write with a broken pencil

how my blue umbrella fails in the sandstorm.
Backlit, the animals retreat from the gaze

of civilized man. Day continues into night,
night retreating through the following night.

So passes a train full of animals & straw,
the dog who ponders where she's going,

where she's been. This momentary road,
our feet at the shoreline littered with Q.

Before the show no father taught my hand
around a peach. I'm a process from weed

regardless, query pressed like a resting place
between circus & circumference. This train

a widow, that other train a ring of fire.
Stoop low, for many are welcomed aboard

dressed in Q. For the greatest flying dog
from Georgia, I have a blinding affection.

On the screen a building falls & falls. When
buildings fall I look as if looking up a skirt,

for there is no beauty like it. I pass a picture
on the stairwell, my name maybe your name,

my name maybe Q. It takes no little truth
to be a brick homemade, to say my captain

treats me well. I pined for news, for a word
swung like pendulum. Like a sequin or screen.

When the first Q arrived, children opened
their hands. I passed pictures in the stairwell

taken in the building, then the building fell.
I looked closely, carried it through my chest.

What pledge in the engine for thought,
what balance in relating the parts. The Q

stands sure as a compass in the woods
pointing north. For he wields a mighty ax,

our secretary can't keep a sentence known
or unknown. Bring out the bombshell,

those zebras concealed in a white dust
& brick. If he smiles, his lips are a lamp

rubbed clean, his speech like numbers
traversing the night by train. This world

little notes nor considers what we say,
leaflets falling countless for the streets.

A hand that held my own let go my clutch
like a shovel. Freshly dug, Q was the nest

for those who'd fallen, the aerialists intrepid.
In an emergency tie the sheets finely: flute,

flue or flurry, one of these does not belong.
No one said pushing, no one said cowardly.

Lifted from our thought, Q passing much
like a pyre downriver to the sea. A terrific

descent through space, altogether fitting
on a great battlefield. Men in lieu of clowns

burst among the shells like columns of air.
Thought flew overhead with a graceful ease.

What sound in what happened, what chest
pushed through with pins, near the center

those leprous as snow. At times an elephant
stands before the light, how light continues

fulsome, house to house like sniffle or plea.
For every drum a sound overseas, the ring,

Q now easier for a camel to pass through.
What uniform, what young man in company

of men, a sweet-hearted man. Close his eyes
like the case on its violin, glance overhead

the Q conducting. The fields were like that:
a glorious wonder, a lake like sulfur burning.

To stand before my captain, bring forth
in a box this country like a Q. First to last,

like a flag folded true, the clear portraits
of a fellow where the searchlights burn.

The building performs a pirouette, mid-air
the second burning like flue or fuse. See also

trapeze, see also the wedge for my captain.
With the donnybrook, I could say also trees,

I can say also Q filled the air. In the stands
some cried out for the implausible heights,

some for that which is great in achievement.
In the streets, some cried for those flying.

IV

In the Manner of All Such Disasters

I imagine the world without tension,
imagine my hands on your never mind

distracted, for the circus carves a ring
by their red shoes, their noses residing.

A feeling nearer song, like cardinals
alongside the window of our bedroom

alarmed, awoken by the broken wing
between my early thirties & notions

my head fits cleanly in a lion's mouth.
I imagine the world without suture,

without memory: I have but often seen
the horse go down & never rise again.

As if god reaches a pair of tweezers
to pluck the unlucky hair from his field.

I confess I'll miss kissing you, down here
kinder yet than a kind of instrument.

My handfuls are curled like flamingos
if flamingos had hands. Impish. So cold.

Sculpture Looks Nothing of Louis Armstrong

Didn't notice the damp except to know
we were in it. We stood outside because

the bridge was long, eventless albeit
Simon told a story. We remembered

to keep the dancers coming, exhausted
where we yielded for bourbon in a cup.

We were tourists, you see. We were voodoo
& alligator heads, the antique mall's

absent antiques. Didn't read the brochure
but we dwelled on matters like empathy

floating a bloated body days. We did
what needed doing. We moved like statues.

Legislator of the Year

—for Luis Gutierrez

If space is limited on the floor of the house,
pleasure is not. Will you check the river?

Of every two Americans, one applauds
over Puerto Rico: payloads bleed the sky,

they're inaccurate as snow. Practice, Luis,
makes perfect on the range of your home.

The stones on this shore are remarkable.
Would you like to skip one? Would you,

if reelected, help my ambition to sea?
Charitable, tax reductive, maybe the sofa

can spare a blanket. We've grown old
& vulnerable. Should these things seem sad

much more is sad: a red pail & shovel
erased by the tide, mystery fastened cold.

In cemeteries your constituency grows:
bugles, the triangle folded so. Gutierrez?

Kudos to you, your daring most tender.
If every two Americans, one concedes

the second term. Maybe we should start
wearing sweaters, maybe our winter coats.

Of this vast lake only the sky recollects
a warmer shore. Will you teach me to row?

Anthem

Ash, mostly. Mostly science, the body
converted to grams, the towering steep.

A stream of lye, the brine as bride maybe.
The first bird against my mirror, mostly

mother's hands & knees, almost magician.
I'm the fool who supposed in forever,

thick or thin, so I imagined some deer
more than or less, statistically spoken.

Weight in a broken palm, calming perhaps
around the anthem. The deer adapted.

I rented the yarn, never bothered trees
fitfully blown & half concealed. The deer

fed mostly on the birds, mostly the young.
I've taken decades to write them a song.

The Last Movie Made in Kansas

If the house requests a hat, she wishes
her brother inside the room of letters

written home. Exit signature, the face,
the dozens who drown trying to save her.

She the ingredient, the house who hangs
in a kitchen of a house. House who falls

where the buckle of a belt nicks the sky
for polish. She who astounds a soldier

on the wind-driven field. Exit spinning
the remains, the spectacle & specter.

If women knit the air past her window,
if in a dream a neighbor sends her news.

In the Sweet Crime of a Waltz

Anna arrives perpetual, basked in perfume.
She wears a fur coat & yes I want, I want,

I want the sheep & count. If we lie all day
in bed we'll never sleep again: Normandy

was murder, Piaf's voice inside the Philco
blazed with pretense for each other's arms,

for tasting each other's nipples, hips & legs.
I put my thumb in my mouth, take it out.

There's no milk there, faces in the likeness
of the train passing through. For every time

I strike a match I take Anna by the nape,
by her cheeks & lips. Rather she takes me.

She's patient beyond reason. Every night
her shadow arrives beneath this fine door.

After Hugo the Jeweler

Until the day our trails become the lake,
our thoughts are far from glaciers, we

without proper introduction, no business
revealing tattoos. We are pale strokes

away from the shore, for a lack of rocks
the professor skipping mussels. Some of us

are married, some dry on wooden planks.
Historically, a dock on a lake makes the lot

okay, tackle & line & our humanitarian
to rescue those confused, those tangled,

those who've warmed too close to the sun,
which burns brighter now than years before.

These friends, these jeweled, always lose
their beautiful shoes. Would you like a hymn

under the trees? Would you like to swim?
The weekend full, wed, we forbid ourselves

the redress of an afternoon clothed. We
think of elsewhere only for a dog left behind.

The fish pursue the reflection & are lost
to our sight. Our lives, until now a balance

of wood & vacillation, perfect if the hour
vowed no end. The water recedes, a boat

stands bleached in the mud, the splinters
of its oar. In our hands is not the lake,

looking from a distance like a diamond.
In our hands is a stem beneath the lilies,

the shudder of a frog, so green, so full,
leaping into the woods exactly like a frog.

In Kentucky Our Families Grieve

The airport empty, I return to a country
where plastic geese slip the night. Here,

the seasonal light gestures, so too the style
when you stow your question in the fold,

the fuselage, through the airplane's course
from a hand. In Kentucky, a fifth of gin

is possession, no more than your river
owns the country through which it pours.

Play the journey with commentary, play it
again from my seat by the door. Seizure

fills the view, followed shortly by the plan,
ploy & plot. Those of my nation are not

as they were, for they stall the mornings
you find arrows, the feather in your back.

I say fifth of gin as if it were the question,
unfit as a fiddle, fire in the overhead bin.

From that very ruin a hand pulls me free.
Before then, I heard dogs barking wildly.

Our Great Aunts & Uncles Are Photographs

If it's true that families assemble,
trial & error of guesswork & string

hung onto air, you soon find a pitcher
finished by lemonade, by oxygen,

your child of the summers hereafter.
Bird in a cage not yet, simply a house

you remember drifting inland, lanterns
mirrored in the harbor like a garden.

Mirror in a bedroom, simply the years
like a sheet, children erased one by one

& filled with water. Beyond an entry
they float on the wall of the gallery,

horizon & sea, the words slung loosely
as if diver's cloth on an empty beach.

Leave us then gently like a kite, picture
of grace they no longer wish to climb.

Answering the Roll Call

To begin the century, to say my name or hers
from California again. What's done is done,

so I want to leave a note for the joy of life.
In bed, under the covers, she says do I ever

wish for death seriously. I say nothing worse
than country that was our home, harmonious

to begin the century. From forest to torrent,
saying she watched the nest balance & sink

through the water by its load. To speak aloud
how the century shifts below the western line

from New York City, the forward stroking
in her chest. Always to begin the century

with this talking of weather. The first snow
of the new year no less than that of a century.

Another Word that Rhymes with Shame

I played no other instrument, both ways
uphill the mooring of entering school.

What is punctuation but feeling paused?
I hung a moment with the trees, sunshine

& dread. I told what I could of the past,
Kansan landscapes, epochs of pleasantry.

How many bushels fit the wagon box,
a window through which as a boy I fell

to dredge memory, the farm's many ponds?
Upon what factors does climate depend

besides the fox that continues to waste
along the highway, splitting these valleys

like a comma? Or my first shooting star,
a part preceding speech, eye to the crack

where I buried my wife, where I myself
am buried now? Early I learned the rules

of language failing, not so much in church
as in the timbre of a creek, upstream,

by which I prefer to swim. So what use
are these rivers, of what use the oceans?

A Small Piece of Land in the Woods

Beyond our spangles & through the pines,
rumors of pedestals, elephants carrying forth

for none. The world turns to sun, seductress,
away again as if on a spit. Some in our troop

are hungry, most are born on the tracks, dusty
& cold where minstrels sing. Our train is tired,

we count the turtles, their slippery pearls covered
in sand. We are not plucky: if we had women

we took them each from behind. Here's a world,
the middle world & climbing, no possessions

but the bellow & addition of fuel. As our dead
disappear by canoe, the last week of summer

enters camp on a mule. She empties pockets,
she casts prayer like stone into the marram grass

where our youngest flush out prudence. There
they find giraffes who rise from a deep hole.

Only then do we kneel to drink from the river.

Also Available from **saturnalia books**:

Xing by Debora Kuan

Other Romes by Derek Mong

Faulkner's Rosary by Sarah Vap

Gurlesque: the new grrly, grotesque, burlesque poetics edited by Lara Glenum and
Arielle Greenberg

Tsim Tsum by Sabrina Orah Mark

Hush Sessions by Kristi Maxwell

Days of Unwilling by Cal Bedient

Letters to Poets: Conversations about Poetics, Politics, and Community
edited by Jennifer Firestone and Dana Teen Lomax

The Little Office of the Immaculate Conception by Martha Silano
Winner of the Saturnalia Books Poetry Prize 2010

Personification by Margaret Ronda
Winner of the Saturnalia Books Poetry Prize 2009

To the Bone by Sebastian Agudelo
Winner of the Saturnalia Books Poetry Prize 2008

Famous Last Words by Catherine Pierce
Winner of the Saturnalia Books Poetry Prize 2007

Dummy Fire by Sarah Vap
Winner of the Saturnalia Books Poetry Prize 2006

Correspondence by Kathleen Graber
Winner of the Saturnalia Books Poetry Prize 2005

The Babies by Sabrina Orah Mark
Winner of the Saturnalia Books Poetry Prize 2004

Velleity's Shade by Star Black / Artwork by Bill Knott

Polytheogamy by Timothy Liu / Artwork by Greg Drasler

Midnights by Jane Miller / Artwork by Beverly Pepper

Stigmata Errata Etcetera by Bill Knott / Artwork by Star Black

Ing Grish by John Yau / Artwork by Thomas Nozkowski

Blackboards by Tomaz Salamun / Artwork by Metka Krasovec

Ladies & Gentlemen was printed using the fonts Kabel and Perpetua.